The authors are to be congratulated for adding to the multitude of recent books on 1 Corinthians, because for too long many have allowed Romans to cast its shadow over this epistle. The authors show that justification through grace, the importance of the body, interaction with secular culture, corporate worship, practical daily life, and many other features are no less prominent in 1 Corinthians than in Romans. For a short, practical commentary, this work is to be commended.

ANTHONY C. THISELTON
professor emeritus of Christian theology,
University of Nottingham and University of Chester

A superbly rich and thoughtfully applied distillation of the major themes in 1 Corinthians. Taken to heart, the message of this fast-moving yet accessible exploration of this Pauline letter will unlock significant potential for Spirit-led transformation and genuinely countercultural Christian discipleship.

MAURICE ELLIOTT
director,
Church of Ireland Theological Institute

T0317069

This wonderful book is a refreshing introduction to the main themes of St. Paul's first letter to the young church in the fascinating city of Corinth. The authors convincingly show that many of the issues the Christians faced in first-century Corinth are very similar to many of the issues we face today in the twenty-first-century church. The entertainment culture, economic issues, pursuit of prosperity, and obsession with sexuality are just some of those issues. Transformed in Christ will be an excellent tool for personal Bible study, teaching, or small groups. I commend the authors for this wonderful resource!

KEN CLARKE
former mission director,
South American Mission Society Ireland;
former Bishop of Kilmore, Elphin, and Ardagh
in the Church of Ireland

Transformed in Christ enables us to understand the relevance of the varied issues Paul addresses in 1 Corinthians for Christian discipleship in the modern world. Ron Elsdon and William Olhausen introduce us to the world of the Corinthians, encourage us in humble, Spirit-led reading of Scripture, and show us the fundamental importance of Paul's message of the cross. They focus our attention on the significance of Paul's teaching on love for one another, sexuality, economics, entertainment (our celebrity culture), worship, and the resurrection.

GARETH LEE COCKERILL
professor emeritus of New Testament and biblical theology,
Wesley Biblical Seminary

TRANSFORMED IN CHRIST

FIRST CORINTHIANS

Other titles in the Transformative Word series

Visit lexhampress.com/transformative-word

TRANSFORMED IN CHRIST

FIRST CORINTHIANS

TRANSFORMATIVE WORD

RON ELSDON &
WILLIAM OLHAUSEN

Series Editors
Craig G. Bartholomew &
David J. H. Beldman

LEXHAM PRESS

Transformed in Christ: First Corinthians
Transformative Word

Lexham Press, 1313 Commercial St., Bellingham, WA 98225
LexhamPress.com

Print ISBN 9781683594819
Digital ISBN 9781683594826
Library of Congress Control Number 2021930746

Series Editors: Craig G. Bartholomew and David J. H. Beldman
Lexham Editorial: David Bomar, Allisyn Ma, Kelsey Matthews, and
    Mandi Newell
Cover Design: Lydia Dahl
Typesetting: Fanny Palacios

TABLE OF CONTENTS

A GUIDED TOUR OF CORINTH

A fellow tourist stopped me (Ron) in the street in Barcelona. "Somebody has stolen my money and credit cards!" she exclaimed. They had been in a shopping bag slung over her shoulder. I had taken precautions. This was a Spanish city with an unenviable reputation: it was notorious for street thieves. Many cities, past and present, have reputations, including the Greek city of Corinth. But was its reputation deserved?

Two of Paul's letters usually command more attention than the others. In the case of Romans, the theological content is particularly significant, but there is little content focused on the dynamic of Christian life in the city of Rome. First Corinthians is different. Here Paul addresses issues that reflect the life of Corinth and the church there. To understand 1 Corinthians, it is helpful to know something of the history of the city. It would be easy to start with Aristophanes, who coined the term *korinthiazesthai* ("to play the Corinthian") to depict its immorality. After all, Paul refers to a climate of sexual immorality (7:2) and expresses horror at a report of it among members of the

Corinthian church (5:1). There is also Strabo's description of one thousand temple prostitutes dedicated to Aphrodite. But the ancient Greek city described by Aristophanes, Strabo, and others was destroyed in 146 BC by a Roman army in reprisal for Corinth's refusal to submit to the authority of Rome. The city then lay in ruins until being rebuilt by Julius Caesar as a Roman colony in 44 BC, probably on account of its strategic commercial location.

By New Testament times, Corinth had become one of the largest and most prosperous cities in Greece. Rome sent many of its veteran soldiers, along with freedmen and freedwomen, to Corinth to avoid overpopulation and to defuse potential trouble, as well as giving them the opportunity for advancement. Immorality in Roman Corinth was probably no worse than one might have found in any Mediterranean commercial center. But old reputations die hard. The problems addressed in 1 Corinthians can be precisely defined. They included: the nature of commercial life in the newly rebuilt city and the art of rhetoric as a feature of Roman cultural life.

The Commercial Life of Corinth

While life in the earliest days of Roman Corinth may well have been harsh, the city soon began to acquire a reputation for its wealth:

> Our survey of the evolution of the commerce
> of the Roman Empire in the first two centu-
> ries A.D. establishes the fact that commerce,
> and especially foreign and inter-provincial
> maritime commerce, provided the main

sources of wealth in the Roman Empire. Most of the *nouveaux riches* owed their money to it. [1]

Freedmen, amongst others, had significant opportunities for economic and political status. They could get rich through cultivating business contacts; they could acquire status by buying influential positions in the city's administration, by giving generous donations (*leitourgoi*) to the city, and by making public displays of religious loyalty to the Empire. The patronage system was a vital feature of social, religious, and economic life throughout the Roman Empire:

> A vast network of relationships, emanating from the person of the Emperor, distributed benefits (*beneficia*) "downward" all the way to the most humble freedman or slave. Likewise a steady flow of gratitude (*gratia*) welled "upward" from the lower social classes, bestowing loyalty and honor upon benefactors. [2]

Oil was needed to keep this system running smoothly. Even if money can't buy you friends, in Corinth friends could buy you money. "Friendship" was the name of the game; benefits conferred on "friends" by prominent people included business contracts, appointment to political office, and dinner invitations—all with strings attached. Seneca said that sincere recipients must "be willing to go into exile, or to pour forth your blood, or to undergo poverty"; this illustrates metaphorically the obligation that bound a "friend" to his patron. Tacitus warned beneficiaries "not to prefer defiance and ruin to obedience and security." In a city such as Corinth, large numbers of freedmen and freedwomen were eager for advancement and the end of the stigma of their servile past:

> It was the goal of many Corinthians, and probably many in the Christian *ekklēsia* in Corinth, to be truly *Roman*, to fit into their society as best they could. Roman Corinth was a freedman and freedwoman's town in many ways and the opportunities for upward mobility were considerable. In such an environment there was tremendous incentive to want to fit in.[3]

This picture also hints at the sorts of people who heard Paul preach and became members of the Corinthian house churches.

Rhetoric and the Cultural Life of Corinth

"I have had my TV aerial removed—it's the moral equivalent of a prostate operation," quipped British broadcaster Malcolm Muggeridge as he surveyed the rise of the modern entertainment industry. This is one of the reasons why media studies is such a popular option for students enrolling in university courses. But it is not a uniquely modern phenomenon. Entertainment culture was alive and well in cities like first-century Corinth; it centered on the art of rhetoric:

> Rhetoric played a powerful and persuasive role in first century Greco-Roman society. It was a commodity of which the vast majority

of the population were either producers or, much more likely, consumers, and not seldom, avid consumers.[4]

The art of rhetoric was prized as essential to a good education, and thus to social advancement. One commentator describes the "debilitating sense of inadequacy" felt by those left behind.[5] Rhetoric became more form than substance in swaying audiences. It was used increasingly for display and ornamentation, and rhetorical displays were often mere showpieces. Stoic philosophers claimed rhetoric had become empty, nothing more than orators playing with style; Philo described it as "shadowboxing."

First Corinthians as a Countercultural Document

These two factors—the desire for economic advancement and first-century entertainment culture—fed into the contentious issues that Paul addresses as he writes to the Christians in the city. He challenges them to see their faith as countercultural. "If a man does not keep pace with his companions," declared Henry David Thoreau, "perhaps it is because he hears a different drummer. Let him step to the music which he hears, however measured or far away."[6] The temptation, of course, was (and always is) to follow the crowd (see Rom 12:1-2). To inhabit our own culture with discernment helps us define the interface with biblical Christianity. On one hand, the economic prosperity that most of us enjoy brings the temptation to put personal wealth before all else, including our responsibilities toward others. On the other hand, the modern equivalent of enthusiasm for rhetoric is a preoccupation with entertainment, driven by the revolution in technology. Thus the former chief rabbi of Great Britain, Jonathan Sacks, writes about "a ruthlessly consumer culture":

> If what children worry about is what advertisers want them to worry about—clothes, mobile phones, iPods—they will not be builders of a free and gracious social order. If public-service broadcasting becomes mere entertainment with a smattering of modish opinions, we will not have an educated, principled public at all.[7]

Reading 1 Corinthians against this backdrop helps us to grapple with the questions: how *aware* were early Christians of these pressures? How successful were they in resisting them? How does this help us to face the same issues two millennia later and go on to dance to the beat of a different drummer?

Overview

This outline of 1 Corinthians is based not on a theological scheme (see "The Theological Center of 1 Corinthians," below) but on the succession of different issues Paul addresses. This helps us hear a two-way conversation: he deals with issues the Corinthians have raised, as well as reports about the church that have caused him concern.

1. Opening greeting and thanksgiving (1:1–9)

2. "Some from Chloe's household have informed me" (1:10–2:16)

3. "For when one says, 'I follow Paul,' and another, 'I follow Apollos,' … are you not mere human beings?" (3:1–4:21)

4. "It is actually reported that there is … among you" (5:1–6:20)

    a. "Sexual immorality … of a kind that even pagans do not tolerate" (5:1–13)

    b. "If any of you has a dispute with another, do you dare to take it before the ungodly for judgment?" (6:1–11)

    c. " 'I have the right to do anything,' you say—but not everything is beneficial" (6:12–20)

5. "Now for the matters you wrote about" (7:1–10:33)

    a. "It is good for a man not to have sexual relations with a woman" (7:1–40)

    b. "Now about food sacrificed to idols" (8:1–13)

    c. "Am I not free? Am I not an apostle?" (9:1–27)

    d. "So, if you think you are standing firm, be careful that you don't fall" (10:1–32)

6. "I praise you for remembering me in everything and for holding to the traditions just as I passed them on to you" (11:1–16)

7. "In the following directives I have no praise for you" (11:17–14:40)

    a. "When you come together as a church, there are divisions among you" (11:17–34)

b. "Now about the gifts of the Spirit, brothers and sisters, I do not want you to be uninformed" (12:1–14:40)

8. "Now, brothers and sisters, I want to remind you of the gospel I preached to you" (15:1–58)

a. "How can some of you say that there is no resurrection of the dead?" (15:1–34)

b. "But someone will ask, 'How are the dead raised? With what kind of body will they come?'" (15:35–58)

9. "Now about the collection for the Lord's people" (16:1–4)

10. Closing remarks and greetings (16:5–22)

The Theological Center of 1 Corinthians

Various proposals have been made about the center of Paul's theology:

- Justification by faith
- Substitutionary atonement
- Union with Christ as a personal experience of Christ ("Christ-mysticism")
- Eschatology—God's purpose as the end of time approaches
- The coming of the Holy Spirit
- God's glory

For any of us who study Paul's letters, the theological center we choose tends to be related to the theological trajectory of the church and/or denomination to which we belong, and our reading of Paul's letters will, understandably, be influenced by this choice. The range of possibilities listed above (and there are others) shows, however, that Paul's theological vision is too rich to be squashed into one "center." Instead, we ought to listen to Paul speaking as he writes a pastoral letter to a particular church. His response to each issue reflects his understanding of God as Father, Son, and Holy Spirit, even if there is no explicit Trinitarian theology in 1 Corinthians. Particularly significant are his references to the cross. He opens up its relationship to ethics, so that the cross is not restricted to the *start* of a living relationship with God. Rather the cross defines the shape of the daily life and relationships to which Christians are called.

> The theological center we choose tends to be related to the theological trajectory of the church and/or denomination to which we belong, and our reading of Paul's letters will, understandably, be influenced by this choice. The range of possibilities shows, however, that Paul's theological vision is too rich to be squashed into one "center."

SUGGESTED READING

☐ Daniel 1

☐ Matthew 5

☐ Romans 12

Reflection

What does it mean to engage with culture from a spiritual standpoint? Is popular culture anti-Christian, or does it overlap with kingdom values? How good are Christians at understanding the prevailing culture(s) we inhabit? What changes have you seen in these cultures over the past five/ten/twenty years?

_____

_____

_____

_____

How has the onslaught of sound-bite information changed our culture's consumption of news? Is this for better or worse?

_____

_____

_____

_____

_____

Reflect on the meaning of Jesus' death on the cross. How does his sacrifice have an ongoing effect on the Christian life?

_____

_____

_____

_____

I ONCE WAS BLIND BUT NOW I SEE

One evening the doorbell rang. Two visitors from a local church stood outside. We chatted for a few minutes, and I (Ron) mentioned that I was an ordained Episcopalian minister. There was a pause, and then the predictable question: "Are you saved?" My doorstep visitors were hoping for a particular kind of conversion experience: date, time, and place. What testimonies often lack, however, is what flows from that experience. The book of Acts has three accounts of Paul's conversion, often called the Damascus road event (see Acts 9, 22, 26). Their minor differences should not surprise us; if they were exactly the same, they might appear stereotyped. Luke's three accounts testify to the huge impact of the Damascus road event on the course of Paul's life. It led to a revolution in his thinking, which became centered on the death and resurrection of Jesus Christ. Paul describes it in different ways in his letters (for example, Gal 1:15–16; Phil 3:12). Such a radical event manifests itself in a richer way than could be expressed by a limited number of words—notably "repent" (*metanoeō*) and "turn" (*epistrephō*), which Paul uses sparingly. We converse in phrases and sentences, not in isolated words. Some recent sociological studies of religious conversion have identified a number of "rhetorical indicators" that employ a wide and rich vocabulary, pointing to the impact of conversion on the believer.[8] These indicators (described below) testify to the magnitude of the Damascus road event in the course of Paul's life.[9]

1. **Biographical reconstruction.** This involves rejecting aspects of one's past life, redefining others, and reassembling the pattern in a new way. This leads to two particular aspects of the convert's testimony: admitting to a mistaken former way of life ("Once I *thought* ... now I *know*"), and highlighting pre-conversion sinfulness to emphasize the power and value of the conversion experience.

2. **Adoption of a master attribution scheme.** This means attributing to one's own sinfulness problems previously blamed on a range of external factors, including the behavior of others. The song "Amazing Grace" offers a good example of this: "Amazing grace (how sweet the sound) that saved a wretch like me."[10]

3. **Suspension of analogical reasoning.** We often use analogies to compare objects. Typical of conversion, however, is the language of uniqueness. Such iconic language—the language of contrast—expresses the sacredness of the conversion event: "I once was lost but now am found, was blind but now I see."[11]

> "I believe in Christianity as I believe that the Sun has risen not only because I see it but because by it I see everything else."
>
> —C. S. Lewis, "Is Theology Poetry?" in *The Weight of Glory*

4. Assumption of a master role. Converts see their primary identity within their religious group, and they willingly embrace the attendant tasks as central to their life. This is in contrast to other situations, where role adoption is assigned by other people (for example, with respect to race or sex). Many people with conversion experiences have gone on to full-time church ministries, some making considerable financial sacrifices on the way.

The Impact of Paul's Conversion as Witnessed in 1 Corinthians

Paul's epistles, including 1 Corinthians, abound in examples of these "rhetorical indicators" of conversion. They reveal a powerful self-portrait of a man whose conversion led to a complete transformation in his life and thought. Examples are not hard to find.

First Corinthians 1–4

In 1:18–31, the opening statement, "For the message of the cross is foolishness to those who are perishing, but to us who are being saved it is the power of God," portrays mutually exclusive responses to the cross. There is also an autobiographical element: the coming of Christ caused Paul to see himself as formerly a member of the "perishing" rather than of the "saved." This is more than a general theological statement; it has to do with the gospel entrusted to him, to which he has already referred in verse 17 ("Christ did not send me to baptise, but to preach the gospel"). Verses 22–24 make an absolute distinction between seeking after "signs" and "wisdom," and the death of Christ, starkly depicted in the construction "Christ crucified." He links this with the two categories of verse 18; those who are "being saved" and those who are "perishing" see the cross in totally different ways.

The section 2:6–16 is full of contrasts: between those who can and cannot receive God's revelation, between the spirit of the world and the spirit that is from God (2:12), and between wisdoms which are human or Spirit-taught (2:13). That the contrast is absolute is clear in verse 14, where one group cannot receive what is from God because it is, again, perceived as "foolishness."

In 3:10 ("By the grace God has given me, I laid a foundation as a wise builder, and someone else is building on it") the term "grace" could be a general reference to God's prior act of grace in Christ or, alternatively, to the apostolic task of founding churches. Paul repeatedly refers to this as his apostolic calling (4:15–17; 9:1, 2; 2 Cor 3:1–3; 10:12–16; also see Rom 15:20) flowing from his meeting with Christ on the Damascus road.

First Corinthians 5–16

One of the rhetorical questions in the beginning of 1 Corinthians 9 ("Have I not seen Jesus our Lord?") refers again to the Damascus road event. Commentator Gordon Fee notes the "vigor" of the rhetoric and the highly personal and emotional nature of verses 15–18.[12] He also points out that the statement "I am compelled to preach" (1 Cor 9:16) is not about psychology but points to Paul's new calling revealed in the Damascus road event (Gal 1:15–16).[13] These words may also echo Christ's "seizing" of him, as he describes the Damascus road event in Philippians 3:12, or God entrusting him with the gospel (1 Cor 9:17; Col 1:25; 1 Thess 2:4).

In 10:33, the phrase "even as I try to please everyone in every way ... so that they may be saved" only apparently contradicts his refusal to please men (Gal 1:10; 1 Thess 2:4). It shows the centrality in Paul's life of proclaiming the gospel. This argument also repeats what he has already said in 9:22 ("I have become all things to all people so that by all possible means I might save some"), where his flexibility reflects the single-mindedness of a convert in sharing his new beliefs with people wherever possible.

In 15:8–10, Paul defends himself against criticism by pointing to his meeting with the risen Christ on the Damascus road ("last of all he appeared to me also, as to one abnormally born"). Two further features of this passage point powerfully to his conversion. Firstly, there is the contrast between his self-designation in verse 9 ("For I am the least of the apostles and do not even deserve to be called an apostle"), and the result of the grace of God ("But by the grace of God I am what I am, and his grace to me was not without effect"). Secondly, the Christ he had previously persecuted was now his Lord, and he received a new commission to preach the gospel. So in verse 10, he compares his own efforts with those of the other apostles; he compares rather than contrasts because he has no intention of denigrating them. His description of his own ministry testifies to a single-mindedness that demands all his effort and devotion: "I worked harder than all of them."

Paul's Radical Reevaluation of Judaism

Elsewhere, Paul describes his former life as a scrupulously orthodox Jew (for example, Gal 1:13–14; Phil 3:4–6). How much remained intact after his conversion? Two texts show that his orthodox Jewish monotheism was radically transformed at an early stage in his apostolic career.

First, the "fiercely monotheistic"[14] text Deuteronomy 6:4 ("Hear, O Israel: The LORD our God, the LORD is one") is reconstructed as: "For us there is but one God, the Father, from whom all things came and for whom we live; and there is but one Lord, Jesus Christ, through whom all things came and through whom we live" (8:6). Paul has adapted this key Jewish creedal statement with Jesus at its core, an adaptation described by one commentator as "astonishing."[15]

Second, in 10:1–15 Paul deals with the grumbling in the Corinthian church by drawing an analogy with the wilderness wanderings described in Exodus. He refers to the miraculous drinking from the rock and comments: "They drank from the spiritual rock that accompanied them, and that rock was Christ" (10:4; see Exod 17:1–7; Num 20:2–13). As with 8:6, Paul has transformed Jewish exegesis in christological terms. Thus Ben Witherington comments:

> The universe of Paul's thought revolved around ... Jesus Christ. Paul's christology illumined his thought in its entirety, sometimes shedding light on aspects of his thought that one might have expected would have gone relatively untouched by christology. For instance, who would have expected Paul ... to tell his Corinthian listeners that the rock that gave forth water to the Israelites ... *was* Christ?[16]

Evident throughout 1 Corinthians, then, is the kind of rhetoric that shows how his meeting with the risen Christ on the Damascus road resulted in a profound rethinking of his entire faith and calling; it was nothing short of a revolution. Far more than a personal matter, it was a huge influence on his ministry and calling, and 1 Corinthians needs to be read in that light. In the following chapters, we hear Paul addressing the Corinthian church on a number of matters, and underlying the text is the question: had they been as radically "converted" as he had? Put another way: were they too dancing to the beat of a different drummer?

SUGGESTED READING

☐ Acts 9:1–22; 18:1–11; 22:1–21; 26:4–23

☐ Galatians 1:11–17

☐ Philippians 3:1–14

☐ 1 Timothy 1:12–17

Reflection

Sociologists draw a distinction between "conversion," in which the person reconstructs the meaning of the world around them (instantaneously or gradually), and "adhesion," in which the previously apprehended meaning remains intact and new insights are joined onto (adhere) to it. Looking at your own religious history, would you describe yourself as a convert or an adherent?

_____

_____

_____

How has Christ transformed your life and your identity? Would you find it easier to introduce yourself by saying, "I live in ... and my job is ... and I am a Christian," or "I am a Christian and ..."?

_____

_____

_____

What happens when church members do not make Christ central to their faith? How and why does this happen?

_____

_____

_____

READING
1 CORINTHIANS WITH
THE SPIRIT'S HELP

No introduction, overview, or commentary on an ancient text like 1 Corinthians can afford to ignore questions of interpretation. The technical term for a sustained reflection on issues to do with interpretation is hermeneutics. Hermeneutics explores the various practices and dynamics involved in how we make sense of a text, so we can reach the point when we can say, "Ah, I think I understand!" Chapters 1 and 2 have set the scene in terms of historical context, author biography, and some of the reasons that prompted Paul to write 1 Corinthians. All this is essential to being able to properly make sense of his letter, but being a faithful interpreter of Scripture requires a special partnership with the Holy Spirit. One commentator puts it like this:

> The Spirit is the One who bridges the distance between the past and the present and lets us see and meet Jesus, the Son of God, sent by the Father, and in Jesus the Father

someone's humility could trump actual IQ in predicting their performance.

The one surprise in the article is that it makes no mention of the most famous example of humility in human history: the life and death of Jesus. Within the context of 1 Corinthians, we are invited to read the letter in the light of a crucified Messiah—that is, we follow Christ's example of humility. That Paul makes a direct correlation between the message about the cross (1:18) and the Spirit's work of revelation (2:6–16) is of the utmost significance and, as one commentator says, goes to the heart of biblical interpretation.[21] Humility is not weakness. Neither is it a charter for allowing people to walk over us. Rather, it is submission to God's reign in the world. Indeed, Christian humility should make us fearless advocates for justice and mercy—even at personal risk to our lives.

Reading in Hope

Inextricably linked with this Holy-Spirit-inspired reading is the horizon of hope represented by the resurrection. The Holy Spirit is the one who holds together past, present, and future until the end of time. We therefore read as hope-filled people—people who follow the crucified one with the promise of sharing in his glorious resurrection. In the church where I (William) serve, there is a practice of reading and expounding God's word from a simple lectern at the front of the church adjacent to our baptismal font. The symbolism of this is enormously helpful because it reminds us that we sit under God's word as the baptized ones, as people who, by faith, have died and risen with Christ.

"The Words of Scripture, by the action of the Holy Spirit, are transformed: they glow, they bathe you and your situation in light. ... The Scripture comes alive. Every sentence seems to be written especially for you, to the point of sometimes leaving you breathless, as though God were speaking to you with tremendous authority but at the same time very, very gently."

—Raniero Cantalamessa, *Come, Creator Spirit: Meditations on the "Veni Creator"*

Reading with Love

No account of Paul's ideal reader would be complete without underlining the centrality of love in his thought. For Paul, the cross communicates the extent of Christ's love: "The life I now live in the body, I live by faith in the Son of God, who loved me and gave himself for me" (Gal 2:20). This self-sacrificial love[22] is the theme of 1 Corinthians 13 as the basis for life in the Spirit (a theme we will return to in chapter 7). It is enough here to be reminded of what is most important: we read as people who are both the object of Christ's love and as those who are, in turn, called to love. One of the ways our love can manifest itself is in our ability to show empathy.

Another way of talking about empathy is to say that we must endeavor to put ourselves in the shoes of the people we are reading about. Biblical interpreters have become more alert to the ways in which our understanding of the world is formed in large part by our backgrounds and life experiences. This insight will make us more sensitive to many of the social dynamics involved in the Corinth of Paul's day.[23] We might reflect on the role of power in the church; the extent of social distance between members of the church; the various networks to which people belonged; how church members actually felt about each other; and the relevance of local and cultural conventions. If we can get under the skin of the church in Corinth, we will begin to understand the obstacles to discipleship in our own lives and in the lives of our churches.

Understanding Paul's Message for Our Time and Culture

The struggle to arrive at an understanding of the text through faithful reading is an essential part of Christian discipleship. When we, some considerable time away from the original events, come to the conversation, we have inherited all sorts of new perspectives, experiences, and beliefs. We struggle both to hear the apostolic teaching and to understand its authority and meaning for our time and culture. In this chapter we have suggested that Paul himself provides some important clues as to how we might achieve this daunting task. We have drawn attention to the importance of the Spirit's help through prayer, thankfulness, humility, hope, and love.

SUGGESTED READING

- ☐ 1 Corinthians 2:1–16
- ☐ Proverbs 1–2
- ☐ Psalm 119
- ☐ Mark 4:1–20
- ☐ Matthew 7:24–29
- ☐ Luke 24:13–35

Reflection

Is the Bible like any other book? What is unique about it?

_____

_____

_____

_____

In what ways might thinking about being a faithful reader
make you a better listener for God's address in Scripture?

_____

_____

_____

How could reading 1 Corinthians in a group from your
church be beneficial?

_____

_____

_____

4

REHEARING PAUL'S MESSAGE ABOUT THE CROSS

"Intellectually contemptible and morally outrageous."[24] Critics raise their hands in horror at the notion of a gospel centered on a crucified Son. Feeding off our abhorrence of violence against the defenseless, the phrase "cosmic child abuse" sums it up nicely.[25] Christians can find themselves on the back foot in trying to justify a faith with the cross at its center. Some theologians have decided to relegate it to a footnote. Given our need to avoid the temptation to offer quick answers, how does 1 Corinthians address this issue?

Paul's Understanding of God in the Cross

Paul's understanding of God centers on Jesus Christ, whom he first encountered in such a shattering way on the Damascus road. Chapter 2 described how this is expressed throughout 1 Corinthians. It is especially evident in 1:17–2:5, where he contrasts the ministries of preaching and baptizing. He affirms that his Christ-given task is "to proclaim the gospel, and not with eloquent wisdom, lest the cross of Christ be emptied of its power" (1:17; see v. 23: "we preach Christ crucified"). Those who respond to the message of the cross are those who are "called" (v. 24) and "chosen" (vv. 26–31). He further emphasizes this in 2:2: "I resolved to know nothing while I was with you except Jesus Christ and him crucified." This does not imply that he taught nothing else; it means that the cross was foundational to his teaching. Paul's trepidation as he entered the city, determined to preach Christ crucified (2:2–3), reflects his awareness that his message was thoroughly countercultural and might be received with hostility or scorn. The wording of 2:2 also has to do with his preaching style: there was no attempt at "lofty words or wisdom" (2:1). He began his ministry in the city "in weakness with great fear and trembling" (2:3) that was, paradoxically, "a demonstration of the Spirit's power" (2:4). Why did Paul stress this aspect of his ministry?

There is not a great deal of exposition on the saving benefits of the cross (unlike in Romans, Galatians, Ephesians, and Colossians), but there are some references:

1. The cross of Christ is powerful (1 Cor 1:17; see Rom 1:16) in the lives of those "who are being saved" (1 Cor 1:18; see 1:21; 2 Cor 2:15).

2. Through the cross there is "righteousness, holiness and redemption" (1 Cor 1:30).[26]

3. Other references include 1 Corinthians 5:7b ("Christ, our Passover lamb, has been sacrificed") and 6:19b–20a ("You are not your own; you were bought at a price").

Paul is at pains to emphasize throughout chapters 1–4 the way the cross throws divine and human categories of wisdom and foolishness into sharp contrast (see Isa 29:14; 55:8–11). There are repeated references to the cross as "foolishness" (1:18, 21, 23, 25) that subverts human categories of wisdom (see also 3:18–20). The cross is "a stumbling-block to Jews and foolishness to Gentiles" (1:23). But unlike Greek or Jewish categories of wisdom, what the cross achieves in the lives of those who respond shows it to be God's wisdom and power (1 Cor 1:17–2:4; Rom 1:26).

In 1 Corinthians 3–4, the human focus narrows. The Peter- and Christ-factions of 1:12 have disappeared; only Paul and Apollos are in view in 3:1–9. Paul is aware he is confronting an ancient form of "celebrity culture" in Corinth, with himself and Apollos as the principal rivals. Having already insisted that the content of the gospel is more important than his preaching performance, he now adopts a tone dripping with irony to challenge them to see that:

- Their quarreling is a sign of their persistent immaturity (3:1–4).

- Building wrongly on the foundation both Paul and Apollos have laid will lead to the shame of having their faulty workmanship exposed as worthless (3:10–17).

- Their quarreling exposes their pride and arrogance (4:1–21).

So far, we have concentrated on Paul's understanding of the cross and his expectation of how his proclamation should have been received. Given his disappointment at what actually happened, what can be deduced about how his hearers chose to interpret—and possibly refashion— his message?

The Corinthian Understanding of God in the Cross

Chapter 1 starts with thanksgiving. It paints an impressive picture of the church in Corinth: "For in him you have been enriched in every way—with all kinds of speech and with all knowledge. ... Therefore you do not lack any spiritual gift as you eagerly wait for our Lord Jesus Christ to be revealed" (1:5, 7). It is not easy to see how this links to the content of chapters 1–4, but the complimentary tone seeks to soften them up before the criticisms that follow. The sustained argument in 1:18–31, contrasting divine and human categories of wisdom, suggests that Paul was finding it difficult to convince at least some in the Corinthian church about the centrality of the cross ("foolishness to Greeks," in v. 23). This suggests two dimensions to the problem.

The Problem of a Crucified Savior

If some Corinthians found it hard to embrace the message of the cross, the question arises as to why. In chapter 1 we noted how upwardly mobile people in a city such as Corinth depended on maintaining their social status in their dealings with others. What would other people think when one of them became a Christian? Barclay comments:

> The Corinthians' retention of their social
> status was only possible as long as others

did not reject them as "impious" or "atheist." Thus some of them may well have deliberately played down the potential offensiveness of their faith.[27]

There are three possible reasons for embarrassment at the message of the cross. First, there was the horror implicit in crucifixion—a deliberately excruciating and public fate reserved for criminals. Paul's statement in Romans 1:16 ("I am not ashamed of the gospel") may also reflect such embarrassment in the capital of the gentile world. Thus friends and associates of Corinthian Christians might have viewed "their conversion from paganism with amazement and horror."[28]

> "Even those who watch Mel Gibson's *The Passion of the Christ* might either screen out the gratuitous horror of it all or be so overwhelmed by the physical brutality as to miss the point that such a death was designed to degrade as well as kill. Crucifixion was one of the central ways in which authorities in the ancient world set out quite deliberately to show subject peoples who was in charge and to break the spirit of any resistance."
>
> —N. T. Wright, *The Day the Revolution Began: Rethinking the Meaning of Jesus' Crucifixion*

Second, the offensiveness of the cross may be linked with its subversive potential,[29] given the dependence of economic wealth and the growth of business on the patronage system. The message of the cross, if seen in this light, could have offended prospective social and business contacts, thereby threatening to damage potentially fruitful economic relationships. Paul's language sometimes echoes the sort of official Roman propaganda that sought to remind the empire's inhabitants of the security, health, and wealth that Rome had given them; Paul may be undertaking a deliberate critique of the empire.[30]

Third, the message of the cross may also have been seen to involve implicit criticism of the Roman authorities for wrongly crucifying Jesus. There are hints of this in 2:6–16, especially in verse 8: "None of the rulers of this age understood it, for if they had, they would not have crucified the Lord of glory."

The Issue of Rhetoric

I (Ron) knew my wife was annoyed the moment she walked through the front door. She had been to the women's meeting at church. All the attendees thought the speaker was terrific, except for her. Great performer, she fumed, but no message. Churches bleed sermon-tasters when they find that they can hear a better preacher somewhere else; these are avid consumers of rhetoric just like in Corinth.[31] What a temptation to listen to Paul in this way! He was well aware that his rhetorical ability was an issue; thus his references to his weakness in 2:1–5 and his lack of "wise and persuasive words." Supporting this is the reference in 1:17 to "words of human wisdom." It is now widely accepted that much of the terminology used throughout 1 Corinthians 1–4 refers to issues of rhetorical training and prowess.

His deficiency in speaking ability resulted in charges against him by the time 2 Corinthians was written, perhaps twelve to eighteen months later: "his speaking amounts to nothing" (2 Cor 10:10). Paul admits lack of training in rhetoric (11:6); he admits that he had not been firm enough with them (11:20-21), possibly because of his perceived rhetorical shortcomings. This is also the background to many of Paul's references to boasting in both 1 and 2 Corinthians. Each orator had enthusiastic followers, who boasted about the attributes of their favorite. The "divisions" and "quarrels" Paul refers to (1 Cor 1:10-11) translate Greek terms *eris* and *zēlos* that were associated with the disputes that habitually broke out between rival groups of enthusiasts. The same dynamic is built into TV talent shows—the judges may disagree, even argue with each other. The studio audience joins in, everyone cheering for their own favorite and shouting others down. That's the way the program producer wants it!

Four "rival" figures are mentioned in 1:12: Paul, Apollos, Peter, and Christ. In a young and immature (3:1-4) church at Corinth, it is easy to envisage quarreling breaking out over the relative rhetorical merits of the first three (all three are also mentioned in 3:22). We have already noted Paul's awareness of criticism in this respect. Something of Apollos' background is known from Acts 18:24 where he is described as a "learned man." This term also may imply rhetorical ability (he "spoke with great fervor," 18:25) rather than learning, and perhaps some formal training in rhetoric. The Peter-party is more difficult to explain. There is no direct evidence that he had been to Corinth, although it was known that he traveled with his wife (9:5); one possibility is that, at least by reputation, he appealed to any Jewish converts who were members of the church. More difficult still is the reference to a Christ-party. Given that this is the only mention of it, it is wise not to opt firmly for one particular explanation. Christ is again mentioned in 3:22–23, this time in a position which is contrasted with Paul, Apollos, and Cephas. We therefore make one tentative suggestion regarding the reference in 1:12 to a Christ-party: was this an exercise in irony on Paul's part, designed to sting them into seeing the absurdity of their quarreling?

In summary, a number of features in 1 Corinthians 1–4 reflect the Corinthians' insufficient attention to the *content* of Paul's message. This was due in part to some embarrassment over Paul's message being centered on the cross of Christ. It threatened the status of people such as upwardly mobile freedmen and freedwomen, who would have been well aware of the horror of crucifixion and the kinds of people the Roman authorities reserved it for. Many had ambitions to rise through the city's social ranks and make money along the way. At the same time, there was a fascination with rhetoric—a major feature of the cultural landscape—and members of the church fell into the temptation to value the rhetorical abilities of Paul, Apollos, or Peter above the gospel that united all three.

SUGGESTED READING

☐ Isaiah 52:13–53:12

☐ Romans 1:8–17

☐ Romans 4–5

☐ Philippians 2:1–11

Reflection

How easy is it for a congregation to be swayed by the performance of a preacher without giving sufficient attention to the content of the sermon? What dangers are inherent in this? How can congregations encourage ministers to increase their ability in preaching? If criticism is appropriate, how should this be expressed, and to whom?

_____

_____

_____

_____

_____

Does the same issue apply more generally to what is known as "celebrity culture"? Where does celebrity culture come from, and what sustains it? Are we swayed too much by the "performance" of politicians without a proper understanding of their policies? Who do we allow to inform our thinking: experts or celebrities?

_____

_____

_____

_____

_____

The cross has plenty of critics today. They accuse a cross-centered Christianity of being essentially barbaric—an angry God punishing an innocent son. How would you reply to someone who threw this argument at you? Does the gospel point to a distant, detached God, or to one who has chosen to enter into the pains of human life?

_____

_____

_____

_____

_____

5

WHY DOES SEX MATTER SO MUCH TO PAUL—AND SHOULD WE CARE?

We invest a great deal in the health and appearance of our bodies. After all, our bodies are the presentation of who we are in and to the world. We think about our posture, our cleanliness, the clothes we wear, the way we wear our hair, whether to wear jewelry, get tattoos, or have body piercings. Our appearance matters, but more importantly, what we do with our bodies matters. This includes sex. Even a cursory read through the New Testament will alert us to the importance attached to sexual ethics from the very start of the church's life.[32] For Paul, our sexual behavior is an integral part of negotiating Christian discipleship. In the context of culture today, this is where the church is invited to dance to a quite different beat of the drum.

Sex Really Is a Big Deal

Sex is not only how humans propagate life; it is also a uniquely precious expression of human intimacy.[33] Sex inspires both the best and the worst of human behavior. The worst is reported in the news daily. Rape is used as a weapon of war. Human trafficking, domestic and institutional abuse, and the mass market for pornography are prominent examples of humanity's moral confusion and failure to respect the dignity and sacredness of the human body. Sex, wonderful gift though it is, brings much heartache. When it comes to sexual encounters, many of us have a track record of failure and hurt. We have either made bad choices or, worse, been on the receiving end of bad choices.

Sex Was a Big Deal in Corinth Too

Our own culture is not so different from the culture in which the Corinthian church found itself. According to Gordon Fee, the reason for sexual immorality appearing so prominently in the various New Testament vice lists is not because Christians were obsessed with sex but precisely because of its "prevalence in the culture, and the difficulty the early church experienced with its Gentile converts breaking with their former ways, which they did not consider immoral."[34]

As with other issues addressed in the letter, we only get to hear Paul's teaching because the church was making mistakes. As chapter 5 opens, we can almost hear the exasperation in Paul's words: "It is actually reported that there is sexual immorality among you" (1 Cor 5:1).[35] In the same passage, Paul suggests that willful and continued sexual immorality jeopardizes a person's salvation (5:5; see 6:10). Further on, Paul exhorts the church to "flee from sexual immorality" (6:18). We will see that, for Paul, the gospel invites us to view our bodies from the perspective of our destiny as a participant both in Christ's death and his resurrection. So, why did Paul believe what we do with our body matters so much to God?

Paul's Theology of the Body

To understand why Paul opposes sexual immorality, we need to first understand the importance attached by the whole biblical story to our bodies. The Bible sees the human person as an indivisible unity of body and soul. As priest and theologian Raniero Cantalamessa puts it, "A human being does not have a body; a human being is a body."[36]

The soul is often described in terms of heart and mind. While matters of the heart and mind are clearly relevant to sexuality, as we shall see, it was the Corinthians' failure to attach sufficient value to the physical body that prompts Paul's pastoral guidance on sexual immorality. He addresses, therefore, various relationship scenarios: a case of incest (5:1–8), having sex with prostitutes (6:15–16), adultery, male prostitutes, sex between men (6:9–10), and the status of marriage and the place of celibacy (chapter 7).

The point at issue for Paul was the misuse (as he saw it) of church members' bodies in the light of their confession "Jesus is Lord": "The body ... is not meant for sexual immorality but for the Lord, and the Lord for the body" (6:13b).[37]

It is tempting to read this verse as a classic case of "Thou shalt not ..." A closer reading might focus on the good news that "the Lord [is] for the body." As Cantalamessa puts it, "the Spirit is the friend of the body too!"[38] Far from giving us a low view of the body and its worth, the value God places on us could not be higher, as we shall see.

Bad Theology Can Be Bad for Your (Bodily) Health

While it may not have been the only reason for sexual immorality in the Corinthian church, faulty spirituality was certainly part of the problem: "Food is meant for the stomach and the stomach for food" (6:13). Paul is probably repeating back this slogan to those in the church who are themselves using it as justification for their current sexual practices: "Sex is meant for the body and the body for sex." What this betrays is an approach to spirituality strongly influenced by the tendency in Greek thought to draw a clear distinction between the material (bodies) and the immaterial (souls).

This belief in a division between body and soul, between the material and spiritual, continues to influence how many of us think today. Other currents in modern Western culture only make our present moral context more complex. For instance, there has been an increasing tendency to think in terms of public and private space so that we can believe it is acceptable to have a public and a private way of behaving: "If I'm not breaking the law or harming anyone, it's OK." Equally, a culture of rights reinforces the idea that we can do what we like with our own bodies—because I am exercising *my right*! But this is a quite different way of approaching intimacy and sex compared to the one we find in the New Testament and here in 1 Corinthians.

> "We cannot think seriously about sex without the unseen presence of God. Whatever our histories we want to be able to feel that our actions have been justifiable, moral and defensible 'in the sight of heaven.' We are right to want this, for sex is significant. Sex cannot be understood as a self-contained topic of ethics, let alone of Christian ethics. It can be understood only as a part of the great story of men, women and God."
>
> —Christopher Ash, *Marriage: Sex in the Service of God*

Sexual immorality might become visible in our bodily actions but, as Jesus explained to the crowds in the Sermon on the Mount (Matt 5:28), actions cannot be separated from the wrongly directed desires of our hearts and minds. I came across a good example of this just recently. Under the headline "Red light moment," *The Economist* magazine drew attention to the rise in people accessing online pornography during the early stages of the COVID-19 pandemic.[39]

Our Bodies Do Not Belong to Us

Paul explains that the believer's body (including heart and mind!) no longer belongs to them but to Christ: "The body, however, is not meant for sexual immorality but for the Lord, and the Lord for the body. By his power God raised the Lord from the dead, and he will raise us also. *Do you not know that your bodies are members of Christ himself?* (6:13–15, emphasis added).

Far from our souls somehow detaching from our bodies at death and floating off into heaven, our bodies (body and soul) await the resurrection and a new, Spirit-transformed body (15:44). In chapter 8, we explore the resurrection in more detail, but here it is sufficient to connect the destiny of our bodies (albeit transformed and made fit for eternity) with the life, death, and resurrection of Jesus. In effect, Paul is reminding the church of the full scope of salvation. If we want to share in the resurrection, there needs to be a death to all those practices and ways of being that are out of step with resurrection and life in the Spirit.

It makes sense, therefore, to make the right choices about our bodies in the present because while there is discontinuity between our current bodies and our future resurrection bodies, there is also continuity: it will still be you and me. These choices are often difficult, and we may well get things wrong at times. That is why Paul recognizes the importance of Christian community, Christ-like pastoral care, and the presence of the Holy Spirit working together to ensure the best support for the believer.

The Body Is the Temple of the Holy Spirit

The same Spirit who will animate our resurrection bodies is already present and at work in the body of the church and, since Pentecost, in the body of every believer. For Paul, this had become a reality when Ananias prayed with him (Acts 9:17).And so here in his teaching against sexual immorality Paul asks the Corinthians, "Do you not know that your bodies are temples of the Holy Spirit, who is in you, whom you have received from God?"(6:19). Paul is presenting the church with a solemn and quite extraordinary insight: by our actions we can make our bodies (ourselves) inhospitable to the Spirit—God's presence. Cantalamessa has written this:

> Almost every time that Saint Paul speaks of purity, he speaks of it in relation to the Holy Spirit. He says, for example, that if someone indulges in fornication (sexual immorality), he sins against his own body, and therefore against the Holy Spirit, because the body is the temple of the Spirit.[40]

Cantalamessa's conclusion is that "we need to take the struggle to live in purity very, very seriously."[41] With this word of warning, it is also important to keep in mind Fee's encouraging comment that the "presence of the Spirit in [the believer's] bodily existence is God's affirmation of the body."[42]

What We Do with Our Bodies Matters

In summary, there are four distinct elements in Paul's theology of the body. Firstly, he reminds the church that our bodies have been bought at a price. The reference here is clearly to the cross. Whatever our way of viewing the atonement might be, our bodies must be of infinite value to God, who did not hold back the life of his own Son to bring us back under his care. Secondly, the metaphor of payment alerts us to a truth we can easily miss: our bodies now belong to God ("the Lord is for the body"). Thirdly, the Holy Spirit now lives in the community of the church and in the heart of every member of the church. Fourthly, and so finally, because we belong to the Lord, our bodies will share in Christ's resurrection.

These four elements in Paul's theology of the body are themselves bracketed within the great bookends of Scripture: creation and new creation. As we have seen, there are ethical implications for this understanding of the body. We are invited to dance to a different beat. Fee puts it like this:

> In an age in which ethics is too often modified to fit one's present cultural existence ... these words need once more to be heard distinctly in the church. Christ has died for us not simply to give us passage to heaven but to re-create us in his own image, so that both individually and corporately we may express the character of God by the way we live in a world whose behavior is "polished nice" but which lacks the purity and truth of the gospel.[43]

For Paul, then, there is an organic relationship between salvation and the subsequent actions of our bodies. What we do with our bodies really matters. If we can begin to absorb this cross-shaped wisdom and act on it, we shall certainly know something of the cost of discipleship, but we shall also know the benefits too. The narrower path will not be easy to travel, but it holds out the promise of transformation in the lives of believers and in the lives of our church communities.

> **SUGGESTED READING**
>
> ☐ 1 Corinthians 5–7
>
> ☐ Romans 12:1–21
>
> ☐ Ephesians 5:1–19
>
> ☐ Song of Songs

Reflection

The topic of sexual morality can be extremely difficult for many of us to address with others. In what ways has the church made mistakes in its pastoral care of people in this regard?

_____

_____

_____

_____

How do you understand holiness, and do you think holiness is important for the Christian life?

_____

_____

_____

_____

How do you think Paul's theology of the body could be a better way of approaching sexual ethics? What resources has God provided to assist us as we travel the narrow path of holiness in regard to sexual morality?

_____

_____

_____

_____

6

THE CHALLENGE
OF ECONOMIC
SELF-INTEREST

I was feeling frustrated when I wrote this some years ago
in a church newspaper: "Why do churches struggle for
money when many church members can afford to buy
second homes?"

In the church where I once led a Bible study group, we
tackled a course on Christian fellowship that emphasized
mutual love, commitment, and accountability. When we
came to our finances—our answerability to each other in
how we spend our money—we hit a brick wall. The late
David Watson once recounted the impact of the charismatic movement on his church in York; the brick wall
was in the same place. When Paul deals in chapters 8–10
with the issue of meat sacrificed to idols, the issue is not
greatly different; the dynamics of Christian fellowship
and mutual accountability can clash with economic aspirations. In 1989, my church minister's wife called me,
annoyed that I had resigned my university lectureship.
She assumed I was going to a better-paid job. In fact, I
left to take up lesser-paid work in a mission organization.

As 1 Corinthians 8 opens ("Now about food sacrificed to idols …"), Paul turns to another issue the church asked him about. It is easy to see this as simply a religious issue, since the prohibition of idolatry goes back to the Ten Commandments (Exod 20:4; Deut 5:8). Paul's next words are: "We know that 'We all possess knowledge' " (8:1b). Again, it is tempting to see this in religious terms only, since "knowledge" (Greek: *gnōsis*) is one of the gifts of the Holy Spirit (12:8). It sounds, however, like a quote from the church in Corinth, defending the practice of eating meat sacrificed to idols: "We now know that idols have no real existence and that there is only one God; so there is nothing wrong with eating meat sacrificed to what others may think of as 'idols' or other gods." If it were a matter simply of abstract theology, Paul might have congratulated them. He finds common ground with them in recasting the Jewish Shema: "Yet for us there is but one God, the Father, from whom all things came and for whom we live; and there is but one Lord, Jesus Christ, through whom all things came and through whom we live" (8:6).

In practical terms, however, this means that it is not enough for them to affirm that there is only one God; it is also a matter of understanding what sort of God he is. A preliminary question arises: why did they raise the issue? The answer lies in the economic life of Corinth, an issue we visited in chapter 1. Particularly important here was the strategic importance of the pagan temples; sacrificial meat was eaten at dinners held there. Attendance was required of those holding public office; others climbing the social ladder were eager for invitations. These occasions were vital for cultivating economic opportunities as well as maintaining social contacts. Christians were faced with a dilemma; it is easy to imagine a reluctance to face the economic cost of refusing to participate in such meals. I contrast this with a young ordained minister I once helped to train. A computer expert before ordination, he could have commanded a salary way beyond what he now earns. I estimate the difference over a lifetime of two million dollars. So Paul's agreement with them is not unconditional; he now qualifies it in a number of important ways. He draws their attention to four arguments: the impact of their behavior on "weaker" Christians, the example of his own lifestyle, the reality of temptation, and the dynamic of Christian fellowship. He does this at some length, in guidance that extends to the end of chapter 10.

> Ron Sider's book *Rich Christians in an Age of Hunger* was published in 1978. Despite a dramatic reduction in world hunger since then, 34,000 children still die daily of starvation and preventable disease, and 1.3 billion people worldwide remain in abject poverty. Liberals blame constrictive social and economic policy, while conservatives blame morally reprehensible individual choices.

Remember the Weaker Brother (1 Corinthians 8)

After the theology of verses 1–6, verse 7 introduces his first argument quite abruptly: "But not everyone possesses this knowledge." There are some whose conscience is "weak" on matters such as meat sacrificed to idols, but they are not to be disregarded; the freedom of some to participate in pagan feasts must not be a stumbling block to others (v. 9). The behavior of the "strong" must not override the conscience of the "weak," for whom Christ had also died (v.11); otherwise this weaker brother may be "destroyed by your knowledge" (v. 11) and fall into sin (v. 13). This also throws light on the Jerusalem Council edict, addressing the issue of admitting gentile believers into the church (Acts 15). Some insisted on circumcision and full observance of the Mosaic law, but after listening to the testimony of Paul and Barnabas, the letter they sent to Antioch contained a restricted proviso:

> It seemed good to the Holy Spirit and to us not to burden you with anything beyond the following requirements: You are to abstain from food sacrificed to idols, from blood, from the meat of strangled animals and from sexual immorality. You will do well to avoid these things. Farewell. (Acts 15:28–29)

This can be seen as an unconditional embargo on eating meat sacrificed to idols; however, at this critical stage in the developing relationship between Jewish and gentile Christians, Jewish consciences had to be accommodated. It is therefore likely that this edict was a *temporary* requirement appropriate to the early church.[44] The issue remained a live one. Christ's words to the church at Pergamum describe how some Christians there continued to eat meat sacrificed to idols ("the teaching of Balaam," Rev 2:14); similar words are addressed to the church at Thyatira (Rev 2:20). Clearly the clash with economic self-interest remained.

The Example of Paul's Lifestyle
(1 Corinthians 9)

Chapter 9 begins the second argument with a series of rhetorical questions (1 Cor 9:1-8), some directly auto-biographical ("Have I not seen Jesus our Lord?", v. 1), others using metaphors ("Who serves as a soldier at his own expense? Who plants a vineyard and does not eat its grapes? Who tends a flock and does not drink the milk?", v. 7). They all point to Paul's lifestyle while living among them; Acts 18:11 refers to a period of at least eighteen months that he is there. As the one who first brought the gospel to them, he might have felt entitled to their financial support ("Is it too much if we reap a material harvest from you?", 9:11). But he deliberately chooses not to insist upon this, perceiving the need for a lifestyle presenting no hindrance to the progress of the gospel (9:19-23). In the same way, he implies that the freedom of some Corinthians to eat meat sacrificed to idols cannot ignore the consciences of others in such a sensitive matter.

Beware of Temptation
(1 Corinthians 10:1-14)

A third argument concerns the temptation to sin. Paul recalls an incident from Old Testament history when people rescued from slavery in Egypt later perished in the desert because of their disobedience. Despite the miraculous provision of manna and water (10:3-4; see Exod 16:4-30; 17:1-7; Num 20:2-13), they still descended into immorality, idolatry, and grumbling (10:7-9). The result was God's judgment leading to death (10:5, 9). Paul chooses this particular example because at its heart was their craving for meat (Num 11:4, 13); the parallel with sacrificial meat in pagan temple meals is uncomfortable. We can hear them grumbling at him: "These feasts are important to our economic ambitions and social position; we resent you for trying to stop us!" In the case of Israel in the desert, however, grumbling people sinned and suffered judgment; it is Paul's wish that the Corinthians avoid a similar fate.

The Dynamic of Christian Fellowship (1 Corinthians 10:15–22)

This fourth argument has to do with the dynamic of Christian fellowship. It is one of the few references to the Lord's Supper in Paul's letters (see also 11:17–34), but it is less about theology than about the worshipers themselves and their "participation" (many translations use the word "fellowship"; Greek *koinōnia*), leading to the contrast between participation in the Lord's Supper and participation in pagan feasts. In order to keep them sympathetic, he poses seven rhetorical questions:

1. "Is not the cup of thanksgiving for which we give thanks a participation in the blood of Christ?" (1 Cor 10:16)

2. "And is not the bread that we break a participation in the body of Christ?" (v. 16)

3. "Do not those who eat the sacrifices participate in the altar?" (v. 18)

4. "Do I mean then that food sacrificed to an idol is anything?" (v. 19)

5. "Or that an idol is anything?" (v. 19)

6. "Are we trying to arouse the Lord's jealousy?" (v. 22)

7. "Are we stronger than he?" (v. 22)

That Paul invests so much in a range of arguments concerning participation in pagan feasts is significant. As 8:1 begins, he already plans the uncompromising tone of 10:16-22. But how, he wonders, do I prepare them for a conclusion that will deflate them? Each argument helps to soften them up in what is almost a "good cop/bad cop" sequence. By the time 10:16 is reached, he has prepared them for the punch line: "You cannot drink the cup of the Lord and the cup of demons too; you cannot have a part in both the Lord's table and the table of demons" (10:21). In 8:1-13, the wounded conscience of the weaker brother was in view to start with; here it is the clash between two principalities, starkly contrasted as "the Lord's table and the table of demons." Even then, rather than deliver a simple knockout punch, the rhetorical questions already noted serve an important function: it is as if Paul is saying to them, "You knew I was going to say something like this in the end, didn't you? Think it through and I'm sure you will agree with me!"

It is easy (but wrong) to see the Lord's Supper (Eucharist, Holy Communion, Mass) as simply a private meeting with the crucified and risen Lord, but Paul here describes a corporate dynamic ("Because there is one loaf, we, who are many, are one body, for we all share one loaf," 10:17) in words embodied in many modern eucharistic liturgies. It is the Christian family, united in love and mutual obligation, which gathers at this meal. Fellowship is damaged when we act in ways that negatively impact the lives of fellow worshipers because of unthinking self-interest. It is this attitude that arouses the Lord's anger (v. 22) in a way similar to Israel's experience in the wilderness (vv. 5, 10). Paul writes this way because he is confident that they will see the error of their ways and not fall under judgment.

A Contradictory Summing Up? (1 Corinthians 10:23–30)

Verses 23–28 summarize the ground traveled since the beginning of chapter 8. What follows, however, appears to be contradictory: "For why is my freedom being judged by another's conscience? If I take part in the meal with thankfulness, why am I denounced because of something I thank God for?" (10:29b, 30). If this is Paul's personal position, it would be contradictory indeed, nullifying all the previous arguments. If Paul has thought carefully about what he is saying to them, this reads instead as a summary of the Corinthian position restated as a rhetorical question,[45] in which he is asking: "Now you can see my position in this matter. This is how you should think things out and come to the right and loving answers to your own questions, shouldn't you?" The potential conflict between economic self-interest and the shape of Christian discipleship surfaces in every age. It surfaced in Corinth in a particular way, revealed in the detail of Paul's treatment. We will consider this further in our final chapter.

His use of rhetorical questions, inviting them to examine the issues carefully, highlights also how easy it is to adopt a lazy faith in which we wait for our preachers and pastors to tell us what to believe and what to do. Students often expect something similar of their lecturers. There are sad stories of churches that have disintegrated as a result. Stories of the abuse of power by charismatic leaders are numerous, and there are echoes here also of the opening chapters of 1 Corinthians, where preachers were celebrities and where performance counted for more than content. As a young Christian, I (Ron) sat at the feet of one of the finest preachers in the Church of England. He said regularly from the pulpit, "Listen with your Bibles open. Think for yourselves about whether your preacher is right or not." Wise words indeed!

SUGGESTED READING

☐ Numbers 11

☐ Haggai 1

☐ Matthew 6

☐ Romans 14

☐ Philippians 2:1–11; 4:1–13

☐ 1 Timothy 6

☐ Revelation 2–3

Reflection

Does the shape of Christian discipleship ever threaten our lifestyles, affluence, or possessions? Does the church to which you belong provide teaching on a Christian approach to these issues? What mutual support can Christians provide for each other in this area? What stops you from doing more?

_____

_____

_____

_____

_____

Consider your own ambitions and hopes for the future: are they consistent with the values of the kingdom of God? What ambitions have you considered that involve *using* money and possessions rather than simply your enjoyment of them?

_____

_____

_____

_____

_____

7

THE SPIRIT IN CHRISTIAN WORSHIP AND SERVICE

Our own country of Ireland has abandoned organized Christian religion in large numbers, but an attachment to spirituality persists for many. From druidic sites to Marian shrines and grottos, Celtic crosses, high towers, and monastic ruins, our Irish landscape is dotted with earlier expressions of this spiritual impulse. What is true of Ireland's religious heritage is probably true of much of our world. For people who are searching for "spirituality" but are confused by the multiplicity of options on offer, this letter of Paul's is an important and urgent reminder of true spirituality. Spirituality, for Paul, has to do with the character and agency of the Holy Spirit. This chapter will focus on 1 Corinthians 12–14 as we explore how Paul addresses the implications of what Gordon Fee calls the Holy Spirit's "empowering presence" in the life and witness of the church.[46]

Let us not forget, the church in Corinth was predominantly gentile (non-Jewish) which meant that they struggled to understand the Jewish framework within which the gospel had been revealed. One area that was proving especially difficult for the church was teaching about the Holy Spirit. Talk of "spirit" or "spirits" would have led to ideas and beliefs drawn from Greek religion and culture that were quite incompatible with the gospel. As Fee explains, the Corinthians'

> "spirituality" showed evidence of all kinds of behavioral flaws. Their "knowledge" led to pride and the "destruction of a brother for whom Christ died" (8:2, 11). Their "wisdom" led to quarrels and rivalry (1:10; 3:4). Their "tongues" were neither edifying the community nor allowing pagans to respond to their prophetic word (14:1–25). In short, theirs was a spirituality that lacked the primary evidence of the Spirit: behavior that could be described as "having love."[47]

Not surprisingly, the collective witness of the church lacked integrity, and this faulty spirituality manifested itself in times of gathered worship, especially in attitudes toward the practice of spiritual gifts.

Spiritual Gifts in the Life of the Church

As Paul turns his attention to the place of spiritual gifts in the life of the church, he begins chapter 12 of his letter with a reminder that "Jesus is Lord" (12:3b). As Barrett observes, "It is the work of the Spirit of God to bear witness to the lordship of Jesus Christ."[48] Only "by the Holy Spirit" can a person own this confession that draws together the various threads of Christian discipleship—including the exercising of spiritual gifts. So, while there are many gifts of the Spirit (12:8–10), there is but one giver, the Spirit (12:11). In the same way, there is but one Lord to be served and one God who is at work (12:4–6). Within the Corinthian church, various questions must have been in the air: which gifts are the most important? Are there different classes of Christian? Can a person be a Christian if they do not manifest certain gifts? In fact, anyone who has been involved in church life will recognize these same questions and the resulting dysfunction that can arise when there is a lack of understanding of the proper place of spiritual gifts in the life and witness of the church. To answer their questions, Paul turns first to his famous picture of a human body to explain how a healthy church should be (12:12–14).

The Church Is Like a Human Body

Appeals to the analogy of a body to provide a sense of unity and purpose were common in the political rhetoric of Paul's time.[49] Faced with the threat of the coronavirus pandemic, we are familiar with similar rhetoric today: together we will prevail! A famous example from American history is found in President John F. Kennedy's inaugural address in 1961: "Ask not what your country can do for you; ask what you can do for your country."

But how does Paul transpose usual body rhetoric in service of the gospel? Not only does he set out clearly the interdependence of the various members of the church, he also counsels church members to give special honor to those parts that lack it (12:23).[50] And, in doing so, we are conscious once again of Paul's theology of the cross, in which Christ identifies with the spiritually and materially poor, the weak, and those on the margins.[51]

As we write this, many of us in Europe and North America are being challenged by the Black Lives Matter movement. It has been a reminder of how prevalent and how systemic racism is in our history and culture. Tragically, much of this prejudice has been institutionalized in our churches. Paul's teaching is urgently needed in our own day: "If one part suffers, every part suffers with it; if one part is honoured, every part rejoices with it (12:26).

> "The status seekers at Corinth within the church perceive such humility as 'less presentable' and even an embarrassment, while the gifted ones ... perceive themselves as the 'essential' core of the church. Paul's reaction, **On the contrary ...** is expounded by means of an unexpected twist in the standard political rhetoric of the body. Those whom 'the strong' wish to hide away as second class perform vital functions which the more confident, well-off, or 'spiritual' can never perform. All are needed."
>
> —Anthony C. Thiselton, *The First Epistle to the Corinthians*

The Priority of Love

There is a depth of fellowship indicated by Paul's vision of the church that creates a natural prelude for the celebrated chapter 13, in which Paul extols "the most excellent way" (12:31b)—love. The truly transformational nature of this new "Jesus is Lord" community is seen most clearly when members of the church are demonstrating love for one another in concrete ways.

The English word "love" has a range of meanings, many of which differ significantly from the sort of love Paul has in mind. Bob Dylan made the same point, contrasting the "pure" love described by Paul with what he called "watered-down love."[52] Love does not, to quote a line from the song, "sneak up into your room tall dark and handsome, capture your heart and hold it for ransom." Christian love is inspired by the experience of being loved by God which, in turn, enables the believer to express this love in sacrificial and practical ways to others.

Chapter 13 concludes with Paul identifying three essential qualities of the Christian life: faith, hope, and love. Faith and hope are the essential human responses to God's love for us while love is a participation in the divine life. As Barrett puts it, "Love is an activity, the essential activity, of God himself, and when men love either him or their fellow-men they are doing (however imperfectly) what God does."[53] Consequently, love becomes the touchstone for everything in the Christian life. This foundational piece of Christian wisdom finds expression in one of the Anglican collects:

> Lord, you have taught us that all our doings without love are nothing worth: Send your Holy Spirit and pour into our hearts that most excellent gift of love, the true bond of peace and of all virtues, without which whoever lives is counted dead before you.[54]

This prayer captures succinctly the antidote to the catalog of pastoral problems in Corinth.

Wonderfully, as Fee explains, love "is a word whose primary definition is found in God's activity on behalf of his enemies (Rom 5:6–8), which was visibly manifested in the life and death of Christ himself." He continues:

> To "have love," therefore, means to be toward others the way God in Christ has been toward us. Thus ... for those who "walk in the Spirit" the primary ethical imperative is "love one another." This is found at the heart of every section of ethical instruction, and other exhortations are but the explication of it.[55]

In other words, the way Paul uses the word "love" takes its meaning from the love of God revealed to us supremely in the cross of Christ: "I have been crucified with Christ and I no longer live, but Christ lives in me. The life I now live in the body, I live by faith in the Son of God, who loved me and gave himself for me" (Gal 2:20). This gospel mystery is not only made known to us by the Spirit as believed and experienced truth; it is also the work of the same Spirit to empower us for self-sacrificial expressions of love.

The Outworking of Love in Worship

Chapter 14 opens with Paul making a close link between love and desiring gifts of the Spirit: "Follow the way of love and eagerly desire gifts of the Spirit, especially prophecy" (14:1). Paul continues to explain how this instruction is worked out in worship—the most obvious communal expression of being the church together. Love is always the measure when it comes to evaluating the health of the church and her collective life and witness—especially the exercising of spiritual gifts. To begin with, the gifts are always for the benefit of others, not primarily the one who has the gift. Secondly, then, the discipline of seeking the greater gifts (12:31) is itself an act of self-sacrifice and love because it has as its goal the best for the church body. And, thirdly, the relative value of any gift is measured by its potential to build up the church community. With this principle in mind, Paul holds out prophecy as a "greater gift"—something we can begin to understand when we read these verses:

> If an unbeliever or an enquirer comes in while everyone is prophesying, they are convicted of sin and are brought under judgment by all, as the secrets of their hearts are laid bare. So they will fall down and worship God, exclaiming, "God is really among you!" (1 Cor 14:24–25)

For some, prophecy is synonymous with preaching. Others will insist that prophecy is more like the prophetic oracles found in the Old Testament that were specific messages given for a person, people group, or situation at a particular time. The precise definition of prophecy is not the primary concern. Paul's point is this: what human beings need most is to hear and respond to the word of God. And they can only "hear" the word of God if, unlike the gift of tongues, it is communicated in an intelligible way (14:9).

Empowered by the Spirit

Drawing these big ideas together, we can see that there are some potentially transformative insights for us as we reflect on the place of the Spirit in the life of the church. Firstly, for Paul, true spirituality always attaches to the Holy Spirit. Misunderstanding the person and work of the Holy Spirit can seriously compromise the life and witness of a church community. Secondly, the Holy Spirit always seeks to amplify the central truth of the gospel: Jesus is Lord. Thirdly, the Spirit bestows gifts in order to enable the church to be like Jesus in its care for every member and in its vocation to share the good news with the wider world. And, finally, the church must be defined and constrained by God's unconditional love revealed to us by Jesus and made available now by his Spirit.

SUGGESTED READING

☐ 1 Corinthians 12–14

☐ Romans 8

☐ Galatians 5

Reflection

Do you find it difficult to think of the Holy Spirit as a person? Do you think the church is sometimes guilty of not giving proper dignity to the Third Person of the Trinity?

_____

_____

_____

_____

_____

To what extent is personal freedom important to you? How does Paul's teaching about the church being a body challenge your currently held assumptions and beliefs?

_____

_____

_____

_____

_____

It has been suggested that the name "Jesus" could be substituted for the word "love" in 1 Corinthians 13:4–7. How do you feel when your own name is substituted for the word "love" in this section? Are there things that you would like to improve about yourself?

_____

_____

_____

_____

_____

How does Paul's teaching inform your understanding of spiritual gifts in the life of the church?

_____

_____

_____

_____

_____

8

THE PROMISE OF RESURRECTION

Chapter 15 is the longest in 1 Corinthians, detailed and closely argued. Paul has been dealing with issues facing the church, some raised by them and others reported to him (for example, "by Chloe's people," 1:11). Here he replies to those in the church who are questioning the resurrection itself: "But if it is preached that Christ has been raised from the dead, how can some of you say that there is no resurrection of the dead?" (15:12). Forty years ago, a young man from my (Ron's) church crashed his car. While driving, he died of a massive brain hemorrhage. Before the funeral, I met his father. "I don't believe there's anything after death," he said, and it showed in his eyes. A year later, he too was dead. I have often wondered if he died of a broken and hope-starved heart.

Paul points us, as with the cross, to a God whose wisdom is totally different from what counts as human wisdom ("How foolish!," 15:36). This echoes Paul's stress on God's wisdom in chapters 1-4. Since the time of the Greek poet Homer (eighth/seventh centuries BC), there was a prominent belief that death was final and that nothing lay beyond it. There were also, in the Greco-Roman religions of the time, various ideas as to what might lie beyond, such as the immortality of the soul and shadowy existences of the dead. Only in Judaism was there a promise of the resurrection of the dead. The Old Testament Scriptures promised national restoration and the renewal of creation itself, for which the word "resurrection" was entirely appropriate. From this, the Christian understanding of the resurrection of the body emerged.[56]

Paul's Teaching on the Resurrection

Its Importance (15:1-2)

The opening verses of 1 Corinthians 15 set out the central importance of the resurrection for the gospel that Paul has preached; not only have they "believed," but in this gospel they "stand" and are "saved" (vv. 1, 2). This is not a neutral statement; there is an ironic reference to believing in vain ("if you hold firmly to the word I preached to you," anticipating vv. 14-19).

Its Pedigree (15:3-4)

Paul is well aware of his critics questioning his gospel and his rhetorical style. This explains his stress in verse 3 on the way he has received the belief that Christ died for our sins, was buried, and was raised from the dead. The Greek words translated "received" and "passed on" are technical terms used for the faithful transmission of a tradition. So Paul insists that they received from him exactly what he received from others who knew it before him. His critics cannot accuse him of invention. Although Christ "died for our sins" (v. 3), there is no detailed explanation of the saving power of the cross here; it is stated in a formula-like fashion, possibly an early form of creed that also includes a reference to the resurrection. The death and resurrection of Jesus are linked in the same saving action of God. So this is "of first importance" (v. 3). Moreover, it is "in accordance with the Scriptures" (v. 4) although none is quoted.

The Evidence (15:5–11)

Verses 3–4 list all the people to whom the risen Christ appeared. Some of these meetings are attested elsewhere in the New Testament; the reference to five hundred brothers and sisters (v. 6) is not, but it helps stress the objective reality of what is being recalled. Then follows a startling statement about the risen Christ appearing to Paul. The language is different from the descriptions of the Damascus road event in Acts 9, 22, 26; here Paul, in his disparaging self-description, appears to acknowledge criticisms leveled against him. The unusual vocabulary leads to his planned conclusion: "Whether, then, it was I or they, this is what we preach, and this is what you believed" (v. 11). In other words, the content of the gospel is true even if they are skeptical; there are plenty of others whose testimony to the resurrection they might prefer to heed.

The Corinthian View(s)

"There Is No Resurrection of the Dead" (15:12)

Paul insists on the reality of the resurrection because its nature was an issue for some church members: "But if it is preached that Christ has been raised from the dead, how can some of you say that there is no resurrection of the dead?" (v. 12). This understanding is diametrically opposed to his. Two interpretations of their position are possible:

1. An over-realized view of the life to come flowing from an intense experience of the Holy Spirit, believing that "spiritual" resurrection has already occurred;

2. A view of the immortality of the soul, in which it is released from body at death, thus denying a bodily resurrection. This view has plenty of proponents today.

Two further verses, in which Paul refers to Corinthian views, help to illuminate this issue further.

"If the Dead Are Not Raised at All, Why Are People Baptised for Them?" (15:29)

A range of explanations has been proposed regarding this practice, which has no parallels in the early church or beyond. But Paul does not expound on its exact meaning; the force of his argument is simply that there is no point in being baptized on behalf of the dead (a practice some are clearly involved in) if they are not raised.

"But Someone Will Ask, 'How Are the Dead Raised?' " (15:35–57)

Paul's strong reaction in 15:35–36a suggests that some were questioning the physical nature of resurrection to which Christ's resurrection points. They may not have been seeking clarification but pouring scorn on an event central to the gospel.[57] Paul now deals with their skepticism in four stages—four contrasts that reinforce each other, pointing in the same direction:

1. the present body is a kind of seed, from which will come, after death, a new plant (vv. 36–38);

2. different creatures have different bodies; the splendor of heavenly bodies is greater than their earthly equivalents (vv. 39–44);

3. the contrast between the first and last Adams (vv. 45–49);

4. the contrast between the perishable, which cannot inherit the kingdom of God, and the imperishable, which can inherit (vv. 50–57).

The relationship between the present and future bodies of believers involves continuity and discontinuity. While this might be philosophical speculation, it is more likely, given the creedal statement of 15:3–7, that Paul also knew about the appearances of the risen Lord as recorded in Luke 24. Here Jesus' appearance to the disciples triggers fear because they thought they were seeing a ghost (24:36–37). To reassure them, Jesus shows them the wounds in his hands and feet and eats a piece of fish (24:39–42). These are clearly bodily appearances, which again involve elements of continuity and discontinuity with earthly human bodies; N. T. Wright refers to this as "trans-physicality."[58]

What If There Is No Resurrection of the Dead?

Woody Allen once quipped, "I'm not afraid of death; I just don't want to be there when it happens." For some people it's too uncomfortable to think about; for others it is an unavoidable reality that must be faced. And some downplay the issue by joking about it. We often substitute nicer words for the more unpalatable ones. So "died" becomes "passed"; funeral services become "services of thanksgiving." Even in Christian families, the resurrection may figure little. A church leader from India once preached at an English church on Easter Sunday. He asked the children what Easter was all about. "Chocolate eggs and bunny rabbits!" they shouted, aided and abetted by their parents. He was horrified. "I gave them hell!" he said afterward ("them" being, presumably, the parents rather than the children!).

If death is the end, what shall we do? One of the greatest philosophers of the twentieth century carried denial of resurrection through to its logical conclusion. Bertrand Russell spoke lyrically but with brutal honesty on behalf of many people in an age where religious skepticism is commonplace throughout the Western world:

> No fire, no heroism, no intensity of thought and feeling, can preserve an individual life beyond the grave; that all the labors of the ages, all the devotion, all the inspiration, all the noonday brightness of human genius, are destined to extinction in the vast death of the solar system, and that the whole

temple of man's achievement must inevitably be buried beneath the debris of a universe in ruins.[59]

The gap between a worldview in which resurrection can lead to something glorious and the alternative, in which there is nothing to be hoped for, is huge indeed. In 2020, the COVID-19 pandemic saw large numbers of people connecting online with virtual church services, presumably including many with little or no previous church connection. In the United Kingdom, after years when the number of church weddings was increasingly outstripped by secular ceremonies, the pandemic resulted in a large increase in inquiries about weddings in churches. News media brought fear, suffering, and death into our homes in an unprecedented way—deaths not just in distant lands but uncomfortably close to home. There is nothing like a good crisis to concentrate the mind and strip away lesser preoccupations.

"Three passions, simple but strong, have governed my life: the longing for love, the search for knowledge, and unbearable pity for the suffering of mankind. These passions, like great winds, have blown me hither and thither, in a wayward course, over a deep ocean of anguish, reaching to the very edge of despair. I have sought love, first, because it brings ecstasy. … I have sought it, next, because it relieves loneliness—that terrible loneliness in which one's shivering consciousness looks over the rim of the world into the cold unfathomable lifeless abyss."

—Bertrand Russell, *The Autobiography of Bertrand Russell*

The God Who Raises the Dead

The first major section of 1 Corinthians portrays the cross as the event demonstrating that the wisdom of God is at odds with the so-called "wisdom" of the world, displayed as it is as "foolishness." Here are two worldviews that people have to choose between. The section 15:35–58 presents a similar contrast, challenging those who deny the resurrection that the gospel proclaims. Competing worldviews are again rejected; the God who reveals himself supremely in the person of his Son is the God who raises the dead. What is preached here has implications for humanity; firstly, the raising of Jesus Christ anticipates the resurrection of all believers, and secondly, God's work of resurrection is *bodily* resurrection, displayed as an act of new creation. Thirdly, the final verse of the chapter encourages Christians to live in hope, not in a passive sense, but as motivating an active and joyful living of the Christian faith in a world that is not always sympathetic to it:

> Therefore, my dear brothers and sisters, stand firm. Let nothing move you. Always give yourselves fully to the work of the Lord, because you know that your labour in the Lord is not in vain. (15:58)

SUGGESTED READING

☐ Luke 24

☐ Romans 5

☐ Philippians 3:1–14

☐ Colossians 3:1–17

Reflection

A survey has shown that a significant minority of American Christians believe in reincarnation. Why might they find this an attractive idea, and why might they prefer it to a Christian understanding of resurrection? How might you attempt to persuade a skeptical friend in favor of resurrection?

_____

_____

_____

How much of the New Testament witness to resurrection is about the life to come, and how much about our present life? Is evangelism a matter only of "saving people from hell"?

_____

_____

_____

How prevalent is the idea that life-beyond-death is a purely "spiritual" existence? How much of this is argued from Scripture and how much from other sources?

_____

_____

_____

9

WHERE DOES 1 CORINTHIANS TAKE US NEXT?

New York Times columnist Ross Douthat describes America as "the most religious country in the developed world, as God-besotted today as ever; a place where Jesus Christ is an obsession, God's favor a birthright, and spiritual knowledge an all-consuming goal." But patterns of behavior of Christians and non-Christians are virtually identical, except that one group goes to church on Sunday and the other does not.[60] For the authors of this book, living in another religious land called Ireland, things are not greatly different. In 1 Corinthians we see Paul urging young Christians to patterns of belief and behavior that are distinctive and different. They are to dance to the beat of a different drummer. This addresses two dominant features of modern Western life, now exported globally. One is the entertainment culture—all-pervasive and absorbed by all of us from the cradle upward, mediated through the power of information technology. The other is our prosperity, which is without precedent in the history of the world but seemingly never enough. Together these two features profoundly influence our worldview: our thinking, motivation, priorities, church life, and our dealings with other people.[61]

To approach 1 Corinthians as merely a historical document carries the temptation to distance ourselves from the challenges it presents as part of the inspired word of God. Elsewhere Paul writes of Scripture as being useful for teaching, reproof, correction, and "training in righteousness," essential to Christian maturity (2 Tim 3:16–17; see Heb 4:12). As one church leader has said, "People should not leave church on Sunday mornings disturbed by what they do not understand. They should leave, disturbed by what they *do* understand."[62] Paul is echoing the ethical call of the Old Testament prophets (Amos 6:1–7 is just one example),[63] and much of the teaching of Jesus, ranging from the Sermon on the Mount (for example, Matt 6:25–34) to the sacrificial nature of Christian discipleship (for example, Mark 8:34–38).

How to Read 1 Corinthians

Chapter 3 of this book has already indicated what 1 Corinthians itself tells us of the categories for a proper spiritual reading of Scripture. In this final chapter we take time to revisit some of those distinctive characteristics of Christian discipleship and amplify them in light of the other major themes we have explored. We will then be better able to ask ourselves how this speaks to our own times and how we might begin to live this out in the places to which God has called us.

Reading with Gratitude

Gratitude can be for material blessings (1 Tim 4:4); its opposite is the sort of grumbling that Paul warns the Corinthians about in 10:1–13. In 1:4–9, however, the emphasis is on thanksgiving for other Christians: "I always give thanks to God for you"; most other epistles open similarly (such as Rom 1:8–10). In the case of 1 Corinthians, this is particularly significant given that some of the issues Paul deals with have to do with strained relationships between members of the Christian community. This kind of gratitude flows from an awareness of our oneness in Christ. It leads directly to Paul's argument about the faith of the "weak brother" when others took part in feasts in pagan temples (8:9–13).

One of the temptations we face is to think only of the benefits for ourselves of a decision or course of action, without considering the effect on other people. This applies in church life as much as anywhere else. Am I a committed member of a Christian *community*, or is my church simply a place where I can go for personal spiritual refreshment? It applies also, for example, to the vexed question of wearing masks during the COVID-19 pandemic. The point of masks is not only to protect *me* from infection, as if it were simply a case of individual freedom. It is also to protect *others* from the possibility that I might transmit the virus to them. One exercise in reading 1 Corinthians could then be to ask: which of the other issues Paul deals with here reflect a failure of some to acknowledge and express gratitude for others in that Christian community? As followers of the crucified one we learn to lay aside our own agendas and priorities to learn obedience to God the Father in Christlike humility.

Reading with Humility

In 1 Corinthians 1-4, Paul has taken the category of wisdom and redefined it in terms of a wisdom from God revealed supremely in the cross of Christ. Instead of some Christians in Corinth prizing their own wisdom, humility would have been more appropriate.

One of the problems that caused Paul such great concern was the squabbling that "Chloe's people" reported to him (1:12). This squabbling was an expression of their fascination with rhetoric; sadly, this was what their celebrity culture *expected* of them. Some of them thought themselves "wise" enough to sit in judgment on Paul's performance as a speaker; to them it counted for more than the content of his gospel. So he had to insist on the importance of the message of the cross, even if his own rhetorical ability was less than impressive (2:1-4); it separated wisdom from foolishness. Comparing the performances of Paul and Apollos was futile and simply showed their immaturity in the faith (3:1-6). This issue had to be confronted again in 2 Corinthians 10:1-11:6, showing how deeply ingrained in their thinking it was.

As Isaiah records, God's thoughts and God's ways are so alien to our fallen human ways of thinking that we are dependent on God's help in order to understand (Isa 55:8-9). To read wisely in the context of 1 Corinthians is to read through the lens of the wisdom of the cross, so to read wisely involves inviting the Spirit to enlighten our minds and hearts (John 14:25-26; 15:26).

Paul's exposition of the cross of Christ also emphasized, in 1:18 onward, that the Corinthians' access to salvation and their membership in the church was the result of the grace of God, to which they could contribute nothing.[64] This humbling truth is expressed in many liturgies and hymns. For many Christians today this is restated every time we say the Prayer of Humble Access in the service of Holy Communion:

> We are not worthy so much as to gather up
> the crumbs under your table.
>
> But you are the same Lord, whose nature is
> always to have mercy.

Again, the challenge to read Scripture with humility means that we must allow it where necessary to rebuke and correct us (2 Tim 3:16–17). In the case of 1 Corinthians in particular, one exercise in reading, individually *and* corporately, is to note the attitudes and practices that Paul challenges and ask ourselves what modern attitudes may have influenced us and threatened to compromise our discipleship.

> "As I worked through Paul's text with great care, I experienced an ongoing encounter with the living God—Father, Son, and Holy Spirit. … As I exegeted the text so as to articulate its meaning for the sake of others in the church, I was often myself so overcome by the power of the Word that I was brought to tears, to joy, to prayer, or to praise."
>
> — Gordon D. Fee, *Listening to the Spirit in the Text*

Reading Wisely

The cross was a stumbling block to Jews and foolishness to gentiles (1:18–25); Paul's teaching on sex and the human body can be similarly a stumbling block for those in the church as well as foolishness in the eyes of our culture. Fixation with appearance and health can be a source of deep insecurity: our weight, our height, our complexion, the color of our hair, and so on. Powerful forces feed this insecurity. Whole industries exist to provide solutions: diets, cosmetics, exercise, and even surgery. Paul's wisdom reminds us that our bodies are objects of God's love and salvation; now a very different story emerges to shape how we see ourselves. This, in turn, will help us to avoid negative thought patterns and to prioritize our time and resources in ways that defy the siren voices of our consumer culture.

We can only hear Paul's ethical wisdom in respect to sex if we listen to his good news story about the human body. Only then will we begin to see the big picture and so apprehend his radical and transformative vision. In chapter 5 of this study, we saw how Paul views sexual morality as one, albeit important, aspect of our bodily existence. Paul's theology of the body is important for at least two reasons. Firstly, we may see our rational or conscious self as somehow separate from our body and so be tempted to downgrade its significance. Secondly, we can easily conclude that our bodies are of little value to God. Paul reminds us, however, that we have been bought at great cost (see 1 Pet 1:18–19). When Jesus died for sinful humanity, he did not just die for our minds, our souls, or our spirits; he died for *us*. Paul's teaching on sexual ethics invites us to see the new status of our bodies as temples of the Holy Spirit. This can be the start to a journey of recovering the intrinsic value of these earthen vessels for God's eternal purposes!

Reading in Hope

Paul's lengthy treatment of the resurrection was in response to those who were denying its reality (1 Cor 15:12). What may discourage Christians in testifying to the truth of the gospel today is finding that some Christian brothers and sisters, influenced by Eastern faiths and philosophies, seem to find the idea of *reincarnation* an attractive alternative. Equally discouraging (if not more so) is the advance of an aggressive secularism that includes the denial of resurrection as unscientific. Essential to Paul's argument is that Christ's resurrection guarantees our own: "But Christ has indeed been raised from the dead, the firstfruits of those who have fallen asleep" (15:20).

This hope leads to a brief but powerful closing exhortation: "So then, my dear brothers, be steadfast, immovable, always abounding in the work of the Lord, because you know that your labor is not in vain in the Lord" (15:58 LEB). This does not seem to have a *specific* application; instead, its implications are wide-ranging. Believing in the resurrection here is coupled with the conviction that our testimony to the truth of the gospel will inevitably bear fruit (see Col 1:6; Isa 55:11), even if we will not see it in this life.[65] This conviction is reinforced in his use of the word "labor," a word he applies elsewhere specifically to the cause of the gospel (3:8; 16:16, and in other epistles). Here, too, Paul's commendation of the Christians in Thessalonica may inspire us: "we remember your work of faith and labor of love and steadfastness of hope in our Lord Jesus Christ in the presence of our God and Father" (1 Thess 1:3 LEB).

Reading with Love

Love is the specific theme of 1 Corinthians 13; it also underlies much of the rest of the epistle. Previously, we have suggested that to read 1 Corinthians against its original context throws up the challenge of making us see how our actions and priorities affect other people within the church. Now we go one step further: In rereading 1 Corinthians, and comparing modern life with the specific issues facing the church in Corinth, how does this help us to see how we can choose our actions and priorities to *bring blessing* to others?

One of the ways love works itself out is through empathy, that ability to understand how others are feeling or experiencing the world. In chapter 3 we talked about love as empathy, taking that one step further to understand the people we are reading about. Once we have understood something of the issues Paul writes about in 1 Corinthians that the church was grappling with, especially where he is clearly critical of them, it would be easy simply to condemn them and convince ourselves that we are better ("God, I thank you that I am not like other people," Luke 18:11). Instead, an empathetic approach enables us to identify more easily the issues we face nearly two thousand years later that connect with Paul's letter.

Ending with a Challenge

A useful exercise would be to spend time (individually or in a group) attempting to put ourselves into first-century Corinthian Christian shoes. Then some questions may come to mind: Given the economic and cultural climate of the city, how easy or difficult was it for them to leave behind its priorities and fully embrace Christ? Would some have found it easier than others? Would some have done this successfully, while others found it easier to merely *add* Christianity to their previous worldview? Why might this have been? What tensions would the disparity have thrown up?

Given also that some of 1 Corinthians is about issues of economic wealth and advancement, how far does Paul's teaching echo the teaching of Jesus in, for example, the Sermon on the Mount? How far does it echo the challenges issued by the Old Testament prophets? Then one can go further, returning to the theme of empathy, to read 1 Corinthians 8–11 in groups where it is acknowledged that members have different degrees of prosperity. This might involve a group from an affluent city congregation engaging with others from an economically poor downtown area. It might involve overseas Christian visitors from the Two-Thirds World (perhaps via video conference).[66] An exercise like this could be profoundly uncomfortable, especially for the better-off participants. But how much of our engagement with the biblical text is meant to be comforting rather than discomforting?

I (Ron) have had a good harvest of fruit from my garden this year, because I pruned the bushes hard in the spring. God's way with his people is not very different (John 15:1–4).

Reflection

How good are Christians at assessing modern culture perceptively? How good are we at relating it to the biblical text? Has your study of 1 Corinthians helped you identify other specific cultural issues that 1 Corinthians might address?

_____

_____

_____

If you have studied 1 Corinthians in a group setting, has it helped throw new light on the meaning of the text?

_____

_____

_____

Is your church a place that people come to for private worship, or is it a community?

_____

_____

_____

RECOMMENDED READING

D. A. Carson. *The Cross and Christian Ministry: An Exposition of Passages from 1 Corinthians.* Grand Rapids: Baker, 1993; Leicester: Inter-Varsity Press, 1993.

James D. G. Dunn. *1 Corinthians.* London: T&T Clark, 2003.

Gordon D. Fee. *The First Epistle to the Corinthians.* Grand Rapids: Eerdmans, 1987.

Gordon D. Fee. *Listening to the Spirit in the Text.* Grand Rapids: Eerdmans, 2000.

Gordon D. Fee and Douglas Stuart. *How to Read the Bible Book by Book.* Grand Rapids: Zondervan, 2002, 324–332.

Lesslie Newbigin. *Foolishness to the Greeks: The Gospel and Western Culture.* London: SPCK, 1986.

Anthony C. Thiselton. *1 Corinthians: A Shorter Exegetical and Pastoral Commentary.* Grand Rapids: Eerdmans, 2011.

Ben Witherington III. *Conflict and Community in Corinth: A Socio-Rhetorical Commentary on 1 and 2 Corinthians.* Grand Rapids: Eerdmans, 1995.

N. T. Wright. *The Resurrection of the Son of God.* London: SPCK, 2003.

N. T. Wright. *Surprised by Hope.* London: SPCK, 2007.

NOTES

1. Michael Rostovtzeff, *The Social and Economic History of the Roman Empire* (Oxford: Clarendon, 1957), 172.

2. J. Nelson Kraybill, *Imperial Cult and Commerce in John's Apocalypse*, Journal for the Study of the New Testament Supplement Series 132 (Sheffield: Sheffield Academic, 1996), 78.

3. Ben Witherington III, *Conflict and Community in Corinth: A Socio-Rhetorical Commentary on 1 and 2 Corinthians* (Grand Rapids: Eerdmans, 1995), 201.

4. Duane Litfin, *St. Paul's Theology of Proclamation: 1 Corinthians 1–4 and Greco-Roman Rhetoric*, Society for New Testament Studies Monograph Series 79 (Cambridge: Cambridge University Press, 1994), 202.

5. Bruce W. Winter, *Philo and Paul among the Sophists*, Society for New Testament Studies Monograph Series 96 (Cambridge: Cambridge University Press, 1997), 182–83.

6. From Henry David Thoreau, *Walden* (1854), quoted in G. Curtis Jones, *1000 Illustrations for Preaching and Teaching* (Nashville: Broadman & Holman, 1986), 23.

7. Jonathan Sacks, *The Home We Build Together* (New York: Continuum, 2007), 236.

8 David A. Snow and Richard Machalek, "The Convert as Social Type," in *Sociological Theory*, ed. Randall Collins (San Francisco: Jossey-Bass 1983), 259–89.

9. N. T. Wright, *Paul: A Biography* (London: SPCK, 2018).

10. From the hymn "Amazing Grace" by John Newton.

11. From "Amazing Grace."

12. Gordon D. Fee, *The First Epistle to the Corinthians*, New International Commentary on the New Testament (Grand Rapids: Eerdmans, 1987), 394.

13. Fee, *First Epistle to the Corinthians*, 418.

14. N. T. Wright, *The New Testament and the People of God* (London: SPCK, 1993), 362.

15. James D. G. Dunn, *The Theology of Paul the Apostle* (Grand Rapids: Eerdmans, 1998), 253.

16. Ben Witherington III, "The Origins of Paul's Christology" in *Dictionary of Paul and His Letters*, ed. Gerald F. Hawthorne, Ralph P. Martin, and Daniel G. Reid (Downers Grove, IL: InterVarsity Press, 1993), 103.

17. Jan Veenhof, "The Holy Spirit in Hermeneutics," in *The Challenge of Evangelical Theology*, ed. N. M. de S. Cameron (Edinburgh: Rutherford House, 1987), 115.

18. In Christian teaching this is called the doctrine of inspiration or illumination.

19. Christopher R. J. Holmes, "Learning Jesus' Prayer," in *The Theology of Benedict XVI: A Protestant Appreciation*, ed. Tim Perry, (Bellingham, WA: Lexham Press, 2019), 110.

20. David Robson, "Is This the Secret of Smart Leadership?," *BBC News*, May 31, 2020, https://www.bbc.com/worklife/article/20200528-is-this-the-secret-of-smart-leadership?ocid=ww.social.link.email.

21. Margaret M. Mitchell, *Paul, Corinthians and the Birth of Christian Hermeneutics* (Cambridge: Cambridge University Press, 2010), 58.

22. Unlike English, which only has one word for love, Greek has as many as six or seven words. The Greek word for "love" in 1 Corinthians 13 is *agape*. *Agape* love is unconditional or sacrificial love and so always reminds us of God's love for us in Christ.

23. Commentators have taken 1 Corinthians 1:26 as a clue to the social makeup of the church in Corinth and perhaps the cause of some of their misplaced aspirations and the factionalism that existed among them.

24. The British philosopher A. J. Ayer, quoted in John Stott, *The Contemporary Christian* (Leicester: Inter-Varsity, 1992), 62.

25. This phrase seems to have originated in Rita Nakashima Brock, *Journeys by Heart: A Christology of Erotic Power* (Eugene, OR: Wipf & Stock, 1988), 56.

26. Compare the words "ransom'd, healed, restored, forgiven" in the hymn "Praise, My Soul, the King of Heaven," by Henry Frances Lyte (1834).

27. John M. G. Barclay, "Thessalonica and Corinth: Social Contrasts in Pauline Christianity," *Journal for the Study of the New Testament* 47 (1992): 69.

28. Molly Whittaker, *Jews and Christians: Graeco-Roman Views*, Cambridge Commentaries on Writings of the Jewish and Christian World 6, ed. P. R. Ackroyd, A. R. C. Leaney, and J. W. Packer (Cambridge: Cambridge University Press, 1984), 133.

29. Justin J. Meggitt, *Paul, Poverty and Survival*, Studies of the New Testament and Its World (Edinburgh: T&T Clark, 1998).

30. Ben Witherington III, *Conflict and Community in Corinth*, 297–98.

31. "Eagerly pursuing all the latest fads and trends / 'Cause he's a dedicated follower of fashion," from "Dedicated Follower of Fashion," The Kinks, 1966.

32. Prohibition against sexual immorality is a consistent theme throughout the New Testament. See, for instance, Matt 15:19; Mark 7:21; Acts 15:20, 21, 29; Rom 13:13; 1 Cor 5:1; 6:13, 18; 7:2; 10:8; Gal 5:19; Eph 5:3; Col 3:5; 1 Thess 4:3; Jude 1:7; Rev 2:14, 20; 9:21.

33. Song of Songs is a beautiful poem celebrating erotic love between a young bride and her groom.

34. Gordon D. Fee, *First Epistle to the Corinthians*, 200.

35. The phrase "sexual immorality" is based on the Greek word *porneia*. It is likely that Paul uses the word *porneia* to describe any sexual intercourse that takes place outside marriage. See Christopher Ash, *Marriage: Sex in the Service of God* (Leicester: Inter-Varsity, 2003), 214–15.

36. Raniero Cantalamessa, *Come, Creator Spirit: Meditations on the "Veni Creator"* (Collegeville, MN: Liturgical Press, 2003), 271.

37. Paul could also warn them "not to associate with sexually immoral persons" within the church (1 Cor 5:9).

38. Cantalamessa, *Come, Creator Spirit*, 239.

39. "Pornography Is Booming During the COVID-19 Lockdowns," *The Economist*, May 10, 2020, https://www.economist.com/international/2020/05/10/pornography-is-booming-during-the-covid-19-lockdowns. A simple

Google search will yield the extent of pornography in our societies and indicate the real harm it is causing to all involved.

40. Cantalamessa, *Come, Creator Spirit*, 251.

41. Cantalamessa, *Come, Creator Spirit*, 251.

42. Gordon D. Fee, *God's Empowering Presence: The Holy Spirit in the Letters of Paul* (Peabody, MA: Hendrickson, 1994), 136.

43. Fee, *First Epistle to the Corinthians*, 219.

44. J. A. Alexander, *A Commentary on the Acts of the Apostles* (1857; repr., London: Banner of Truth Trust, 1963), 84: "The abstinence here recommended must be understood ... not as an essential Christian duty, but as a concession to the consciences of others, i.e. of the Jewish converts, who still regarded such food as unlawful and abominable in the sight of God."

45. Ben Witherington III, *Conflict and Community in Corinth*, 228.

46. The phrase "God's empowering presence" is taken from Gordon Fee's major study on the Holy Spirit in Paul's letters. See Gordon D. Fee, *God's Empowering Presence*.

47. Gordon D. Fee, *First Epistle to the Corinthians*, 631.

48. C. K. Barrett, *A Commentary on the First Epistle to the Corinthians*, 2nd ed. (London: A&C Black, 1979), 283.

49. Barrett, *Commentary on the First Epistle to the Corinthians*, 287.

50. Similarly, the coronavirus pandemic has reminded us of those who are most vulnerable in our communities. We have also become aware of our interdependence in society. How much more appreciative have we become of those people who are frontline workers—in hospitals, care homes, or our supermarkets?

51. There are echoes of this motif elsewhere in Scripture, for example, in the song of Hannah (1 Sam 2:1–10) and the Magnificat (Luke 1:46–55).

52. Bob Dylan, "Watered-Down Love," *Shot of Love*, Columbia Records, 1981.

53. Barrett, *Commentary on the First Epistle to the Corinthians*, 311.

54. *Book of Common Prayer*, Church of Ireland (Dublin: Columba Press, 2004), 283.

55. Fee, *First Epistle to the Corinthians*, 631.

56. The Apostles' Creed: "I believe in ... the resurrection of the body, and the life everlasting."

57. Robertson and Plummer put these words into the mouths of Paul's doubters: "Can we conceive of such a thing? We cannot be expected to believe what is impossible and inconceivable." Archibald Robertson and Alfred Plummer, *A Critical and Exegetical Commentary on the First Epistle of St. Paul to the Corinthians*, International Critical Commentary 33 (Edinburgh: T&T Clark, 1914), 368.

58. N. T. Wright, *The Resurrection of the Son of God* (London: SPCK, 2003), 661.

59. Bertrand Russell, "A Free Man's Worship," *The Independent Review* 1 (December 1903), 415.

60. Cited in Gerald Hiestand and Todd Wilson, *The Pastor Theologian: Resurrecting an Ancient Vision* (Grand Rapids: Zondervan, 2015), 53.

61. This is sometimes called the "McDonaldization of culture." See "Cultural Imperialism: McDonaldization," *Communication Technology 101*, February 24, 2016, https://communicationtechnology101.wordpress.com/2016/02/24/cultural-imperialism-mcdonaldization/.

62. George Kovoor, speaking at the Church of Ireland Theological Institute, Dublin, Ireland, 1999.

63. There are echoes here of an older entertainment culture as well as a deadening preoccupation with wealth and luxury. Contrary to popular misconceptions, there is far more about prosperity and economic justice in the Bible than about sex!

64. Contrast this with the widely circulated quip about "a self-made man who worships his creator."

65. The term "in vain" (Greek: *kenos*) is one Paul has already applied to his own ministry ("not without effect," 15:10) and to the Corinthians' belief in the resurrection (not "useless," 15:14). In these cases, the associated Greek word *kenē* is used.

66. This is an exercise that would need to be carefully planned and led. What might simply be an exercise in politeness would not bear fruit; there would be no proper engagement with Scripture or with each other. The possible challenges are such that some participants might feel insulted or patronized by the views of others; all participants will need to be prepared for uncomfortable challenges.

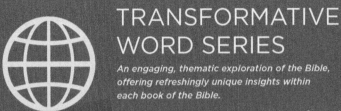